Gary Tharaldson

PAPER

Everything I do is for

Christine, Charles, Regan, and Ruby

Thanks for putting up with me.

Contents

Trey 7

True Love 8

Window Seat 9

That Lady, Right There 10

Why? 11

God 12

The Bosses Wife 13

Pillow Talk 14

Fruit Loops 15

Phillip Morris 16

Two Beers, please. 17

Paper Butterfly 18

Insomnia 19

Salt Water Taffy 20

11am. 21

Existential Loops 22

Look Up 23

The Greatest Road Trip 24

District of Columbia 25

Every Minute 27

Forest Language 28

The Holy Union 29

Before You Doze 30

Be Different 31

Trained	32
Bullies & Trophies	33
Jerry	34
Tough	35
Beautiful on the Outside	36
Let Her Bloom	37
Set for Life	38
Michael	39
Boy or Man?	40
Paper	41
This Book	42
Lighter Load	43
Remembering	44
October 22	45
The Hunter	46
Rush Hour	47
Poor Peter Peck	48
Purpose	49
The Vulture	50
Flashback	51
Go Back	52
Eliminate Waste	53
Addiction	54
Poetry Pause	55
So Still	56
I Killed The Fox	57
Jim Harrison	58
Anthony	59

7's	60
How the World Works	61
Neil's Law	62
Comfort	63
Experience	64
Warm Waves	65
Missing	66
Talk	67
Fly, girl	68
Television	69
Halo	70
A Million Heartbeats	71
Prison Frames	72
Grudges	73
Kind	74
Lost at Sea	75
Highschool Kids	76
Discover	77
Logging Notes	78
Powerful Pictures	79
New Clothes	80
Sunday's	81
1984	82
Spidermom	83
Robert	84
Airmail	85
Outer Crabs	86

Paper

Trey

He was an odd-shaped boy,
head too big for his torso,
spirit too big for his body.
An everyday irritation of endless jokery,
but someone you had to root for.
I found Trey's obituary,
60 years too early.
I hope he grew into that body of his.

True Love

I have terrible dreams
of losing her.
It's usually kidnappings.
But once she just
wandered away from me,
lost in the woods
without the skills to survive.
My mind raced like
a starving rat in an endless maze.
I found her though,
in a fully functioning igloo.
She invited me inside for tea.

Window Seat

A black woman with blue eyes,
wrinkled her brow at me, and with the slowest,
raspiest,
dark,
voice...
she whispered with lip arched, "You're the white devil, with your blue eyes and your white skin."

All I wanted from her,
was the window seat.

That Lady, Right There

He was the all-powerful ruler of the house.
What he said went,
even when he wasn't saying a word.
A company man,
with over 30 years at General Motors.
A strong taste for booze
and an even stronger taste for women.
Born with a silver tongue,
they dropped at his feet.
"I never met a woman,
I didn't want to marry!"
Old ladies surrounding me
at his wake, like vultures over roadkill.
"I was his favorite!"
"We were going to get married!"
"You look just like him!"
A man I never met
whispered in my ear,
"He's currently having an affair,
with that lady, right there."

Why?

Why would any of you
care about any of what I must say?
I am a nobody.
I've never been in a motion picture.
I've never read a poem on stage.
I haven't been on television
or made billons selling real estate.
But I have lived.
I've cleaned the remains of my dead father
I've smelled death
I've served
I've been so addicted to
       making my life better
That I've ruined it.
I'm a risk taker
A hallucinator
and a masturbator
and I care about humanity
and love and giving and
guiding and helping and
defending.

But most of all, I obsess about creating.

God

There is a mythical man,
or is it a woman?
Some say it is the sacred cow
that lends its magical udder to the masses.
Rosary beads lead to devious deeds.
A fat man in a Chinese restaurant
laughs at the idea.
An emo kid with
the pentagram patch
burns matches to fingertips,
and the door to door Jehovah, celebrates nothing.
Believe in yourself and only yourself,
for you, are the creator of your happiness.

The Bosses Wife

Babs was the life of the party.
A short, stout woman,
her make-up was an over-the-top rendition
of flour and robin eggs
with a kiss of fire engine red lipstick.
She demanded good times,
and chained smoked long, skinny,
cigarettes.
Armed with a mouth full of teeth
that would make a thoroughbred blush,
she would party no more.
Pain killers and booze took her too soon,
and our little get togethers would never be the same.

Pillow Talk

Squeezing these lids
I struggle to turn off
the projector.
Who cares about this
orange popsicle
melting down my fat belly
into the top of my diaper?
Yet here it is, again.
Flipping through memories
until I reach today.
Why didn't I do more?
Will they remember me?
What can I do differently tomorrow?
What can I do differently,
tomorrow?
Lids are heavy now.
The artificial melatonin is kicking in…
I hope I see tomorrow.

Fruit Loops

"Well, I'm going to work
sweet daughter of mine.
I love you, good bye."
With a mouthful of fruit loops and
milk running down her chin,
her eyebrows raise slowly,
as does her middle finger.
Lovingly.
Like it was the international sign
for love.
I politely ask, "What does that mean, honey?"
As slowly as the middle finger went up,
it went down again and she said,
"It means I love you, daddy.
I learned it on the bus."

A solid argument for homeschooling.

Phillip Morris

I'm not sure why
I hate smokers so much?
My mother puffed on those
cancer sticks everywhere we went.
Back then you could smoke
inside the mall, at work, in restaurants,
and of course, inside a car
with the windows up.
The stench of minty Kools in my clothes
gagged me during all aspects
of my adolescence.
Burned by accidental hand waving,
camp fire smoldering scents
in everything I wore.
The ugly faces she makes when lighting up.
Or that last massive drag
before walking into the grocery store,
exhaling smog over-top, the russet potatoes
and sweet onions.
Daring someone to challenge her right to smoke,
like those "fucking yuppies!"
Maybe it was because I was forced to
run in the store
and buy packs of smokes for her?
Or maybe it was the way
butts were extinguished on
half empty dinner plates?
Spaghetti and tobacco left-overs.
Nothing good has ever come of smoking,
except for my good health.

Two Beers, please.

Dos cerveza por favor!
My young children
are always impressed
with my bi-lingual savvy.
I've been doing the same
coin trick for years.
My age defines my salary,
not my talent or lack thereof.
This wiry gray hair of mine
earns me respect, "Yes, sir" it does.
A rigorous head nod
and animated arms
can win most debates.
Turn up your volume for good measure
or walk out of the room
on a high note.
Life isn't that hard
if you know how to manipulate it.

Paper Butterfly

The world was created,
we can all agree on that.
What has you
so blue in the face
these days?
Come with me and make
a paper butterfly.
Cry with me
when it doesn't fly,
but celebrate too
that we tried.

Insomnia

One day
I stopped sleeping
and couldn't stop thinking.
These old packets
of splattered ketchup
coat my brand new
white tennis shoes.
Over there,
I cut my own hair...
and was disappointed.
We stayed out
all night long
on a playground in Milford
coughing on cigarettes
and singing songs
with no radio.
A pencil stabbed my hand.
A blue dot on my rib.
I crash landed a
two wheeled scooter.
Meaningless miles of tape
no one else will ever see.
I'm doomed with open eyes
that no one else can see.

Salt Water Taffy

The most boring trip
of my life
ended with salt water taffy.
The end.

11am.

I met a man, in a bar,
in San Francisco.
He's clearly an alcoholic.
Pounding long island iced teas
and queuing music
from the 1980's.
Drinking before noon,
not in a touristy way like us.
With purpose on this
Tuesday morn.
A passionate tax man,
he weaves amazing stories
of fooling the IRS.
He recites many tax code verses
like a Baptist minister on a Sunday morning.
It's easy to see the lonely man
between his stories.
The smoky voice of the bartender
cuts him off before the clock strikes noon,
but he doesn't care.
"There are 300 bars in the metro area!"
And off he went, waving and laughing.

Existential Loops

Nothing is real,
not even the words
on this page.
Everything ever said or done
has been done with the purpose
of deceiving or influencing
your original thoughts.
So, go!
Go now and influence others
with your thoughts and ideas.

Look Up

So many
chained to technology,
their babies suffer
and no one
looks up.
Even in the dullest
of places to live,
the magnificent colors
of sunrise and sunset are missed.
Look at your children,
make up a story from your past,
grab their hands and walk.
Point and tell them to
look up.

The Greatest Road Trip

The greatest road trip
of my adolescence was
filled with near death experience
and cases of Molson Golden.
The driver leaves his
seat at 60 miles per hour
to take a well-deserved rest.
The smallest one
steals a scooter
and breaks his ankle
parallel parking into a brick wall.
Shots of vodka
by nothing but candle light
sends us off to break noses
and bleed too much.
Regurgitation of libations
worn on sweaters
like badges of honor
we celebrate like war heroes.

District of Columbia

Her water breaks
and has a baby
at the famous L'Enfant Plaza
train station.
A woman loses her life
to unsafe subway cars,
smoke takes her lungs.
Oil men walk the aisles
strapped up like suicide bombers,
but armed only with sweet scents.
A bullet to the head
on the Capitol steps.
He takes his life
to protest the 1%.
I wave to Al Gore
at a Starbucks
and thank him for the internet.
In Chinatown,
a man disappears between her legs
and people continue to shop.
A broke down truck,
these men need my help,
but they're already dead.
Mind control is preached
by a sidewalk evangelist
and sometimes, I wonder.
Muhammad walks his dog,
appearing to be homeless,
but is a rich and mentally touched
trust fund adult.
A cigarette smolders
between his fingers
as he sleeps, or dies,
in front of the MLK library.
A paramedic tells me to fuck off.

Cities are made
for visiting,
not living.

Every Minute

One day you won't wake up.
Or, perhaps, your eyes will close
for one last time
in the middle of the day.
There probably won't be time
to thank everyone for the fun
you've had – or to say, "I love you".
So make every minute count,
and for those of you reading this,
I love you.

Forest Language

There you sit
high amongst the oaks
and the gums.
Nuts and balls
on the forest floor,
and all you can think of
is the mighty buck.
A few squirrels
are in charge of the corn pile now,
daring this little rabbit
to intrude.
A fight breaks out
and it's a draw.
The squirrels race up trees
sounding their alarms.
The red fox is moving with purpose.
No one sees the buck tonight.

The Holy Union

There's nothing holy
about it really.
Marital bliss comes
and it goes.
When it goes for good,
so should you.
There is no reward
for suffering.

Before You Doze

The best poems
are written at night,
just before unconsciousness.
Fight the sleepy monsters
that pull on your eyelids
and scribble your prose
before you doze.

Be Different

Indecision killed the squirrel
and it'll kill you too
if you're not careful.
There are two paths
you can take,
and it's not always the one less traveled.
It's right there
through the wall of fear,
you'll have to smash through it.
To hell with your safe passages!

Trained

We are trained at an early age
to do nothing for free and get
what's coming to us.
Volunteerism is a four letter word,
it's fucking FREE isn't it?
Giving your time for
nothing in return
for the betterment
of another.
Untrain.
Give.
Be.
Free.

Bullies & Trophies

Every complaining parent
will tell you,
"When I was a kid…"
But that was then,
and this is now.
When you're 45
no one will care that your
whole team got a trophy for last place.
Bullies have been around
since man was created by cosmic dust,
no amount of "awareness" will get rid of them.
Avoid them,
don't be one,
and just concentrate on bettering,
you.

Jerry

An old man now,
he lives in a house
with no toilet
and no running water.
He poops in a
wooden box on the edge
of the woods.
Tools and mechanical know-how
litter his living room,
which is the front yard,
and the foyer,
and the mud room.
With no cable television,
no telephone,
and no internet,
Jerry sings.
His vocal cords,
in complete unison,
make the most beautiful sounds
a poor man could ever make.
Birds stop and listen.
On a stage in Nashville,
dressed like an old
Harley Davidson outlaw,
people snickered and sat bewildered.
As the first notes pour out,
the people are silent and start to hear.
Eyes wide
and jaws slacked,
a brief moment of silence
and then...
THUNDEROUS ROARS!
 Let your talent take you places,
not your possessions.

Tough

Some humans love,
to be tough.

"Walk it off!", they'll say...
That never works.

"What happened to punching them in the mouth!", they'll say...
Ignorance makes a man clench his fists.

"Do you see how fat she is?", they'll say...
Shape doesn't define you.

"That's so gay.", they'll say...
Love isn't a curse.

I used to be tough.

Now, I just want a long hug.

Even if you are injured,
or opinionated,
or chunky, or different.

I used to be tough.

Beautiful on the Outside

The red fox
is a beautiful creature
with cruel intensions.
They are the serial killer
of the woods.
Every day they seek prey,
and are sly in doing so.
Premeditated, as soon as they wake,
and dreaming of the chase
when they doze in their den.
Teaching their children the
ways of the fox,
like some women I know.

Let Her Bloom

Don't prune the rose bush
that blooms wildly.
She's so beautiful in so many ways,
why would you cut off her arms
to spite your face?

Set for Life

Safe and calculated
was the way he died,
before he could enjoy
his retirement.

Michael

Skinny
and wheelchair confined
Michael

No
we didn't have rules for a
Seatbelt

Forever
i try to imagine
Paralyzed

Boy or Man?

When a boy
believes himself
to be a man
when he clearly hasn't been tested fully,
the results
inevitably
are sobering.

Paper

I can see myself writing
on any corner of paper I could find
that had room for thoughts.
Pencils broken in every drawer,
not a sharpener in this whole damned house.
Gripping a shard of lead I scribble down
my ideas and tuck them away in my underwear drawer
where surely, they'll be safe from everyone.
In those days there weren't computers,
or tablets,
or digital dart boards.
All we had was paper.

This Book

I wouldn't say this book is all you need,
but you *could* read it when you're bored,
happy, or sad.
If lost in the woods with only this book,
I suppose you could use it as a pillow.
Perhaps a sheet or two could
save you from diaper rash.
Paper airplanes fly best
when made of,
paper.

You could write your own poems
in the margins
and share them with your friends.
Prop open a door.
Protect your bare legs from a hot plate.
Level a table.
Be inspired.
Sign it, and pass it on –
and one day I hope to come across your filthy book,
and do it all over again.

Lighter Load

There was a time when I could
tell you the name of the player with
the most strikeouts in the league.

I studied lyrics on the back
of old cassette inserts,
I knew every word to my favorites.

I stayed up so late,
on countless nights,
to watch those music videos they all talked about.

Many years went
perfecting the mechanics of
a driver, a wedge, and a putter.

Obsessed with adult playdates,
outings, and happy hours,
being social was so important.

Speaking of social,
these phones have crippled my thumbs
and given me involuntary tremors.

All this time wasted,
when I could have been
creating and leaving a legacy.

It's never too late however,
to show up for your life
and do what you were meant to do.

Remembering

I've been told that a dragonfly
is a sign that a loved one
who has passed, is checking up on you.
Instant cool breezes on the hottest days
or in the middle of your house, when no windows are open.
That song that came on,
the last time you heard it was
with that person.
They're with you now, as you read these very words.
Point out those sunsets
and those double rainbows
while you are still alive,
and those experiences
will live on forever,
with the living.

October 22

A swirling soft breeze
of long, half curled,
raven hair.

A restored vision of
The Birth of Venus.

Her imperfections
are perfect for me,
as mine are for hers.

I scratch at her scar
where her heart was fixed,
hoping I never break it.

These old hands,
know real love,
when they feel it.

Tiny toe prints on the window,
her smell on my button-downs,
all because of that look she
said she never gave me.

The Hunter

Look around you the next time
you are in a place where humans
gather.

Whether buried in phone screens,
or twitching like chickens do,
they hunt.

Humans are forever on the hunt
for something to satisfy self.

A new book, a tasty recipe,
the perfect man, or the perfect woman.
The hunter is relentless.

Entrepreneurs spend a lifetime
producing game,
for humans to bag.

Be the entrepreneur, not the hunter.

And if not the entrepreneur,
create for yourself,
for there is no greater pleasure.

Rush Hour

So quiet, I was, in this giant oak tree.
For hours I sat, not moving a muscle in
hopes of seeing that giant buck wander into sight.
These moments are few and far between,
but that is okay with me.
I watch the busy lives of animals
swirl around me with purpose.
The squirrels don't feel fall coming yet.
These 90 degree days, in late September,
have them playing and eating
without bothering to gather the crumbs.
A female cardinal lands on a branch
just beneath my foot.
My statue-like stillness impresses me
for a moment.
A regular has arrived on my pile of corn,
just over there.
He's made friends with the squirrels but
still fears the raccoons and ground hogs.
The cardinal is dreaming now,
eyes closed, and breathing heavy.
A single yellow oak leaf,
falls slowly from high above in slow motion spirals,
surely because of this thick heat.
The ants are commuting across my lap now,
and if I leave them be,
I'll continue to enjoy rush hour.

Poor Peter Peck

Poor Peter Peck
hadn't a pot to piss in.
He stole from his mother's purse,
money she didn't have,
to buy the things that
didn't make him happy.
He was ashamed of her trailer trap
she kept him in.
A double wide reminder
that we are going nowhere,
fast.
Poor Peter Peck
picked pockets
for the last time
and joined the Navy,
just in time.

Purpose

Our purpose is strong at a young age. "Learn your ABC's and get that degree!" The gold standard for many years was the 6 digit salary. To what purpose? Congratulations, you've made it to financial prison! Have a seat over there on your utility bills and that mortgage the bank says you *can* afford. But why be negative in all this? Purpose comes and goes doesn't it? Wipe this paragraph from your mind, and read this instead:

Live small so you can sleep at night and love those closest to you.

The Vulture

High above the tree tops
deep in the forest
and on the forest floor
a dark shadow circles.
The laziest animal
in the woods,
mocks the wounded
and feasts on the deceased.
Like some corporate types
I know.

Flashback

Tell me your recollection
of 1974.
I say, "I saw me in my underwear."
There, I see it now.
Grainy film,
barely developed,
like an old faded Polaroid.
The flash sticks
operate magically
like nothing I've seen before.

Go Back

The woods will swallow you up quickly,
if you're not careful.
Every tree looks like the last
and when you start to spin,
you'll lose your way.
Lost forever in someone's mess.
Don't trust just any tree you see.
Talk to it, and let it know you care,
just to see if it reciprocates your tenderness.
Sprinkle crumbs, tie ribbons, and hold on
to the path that led you here.

Eliminate Waste

The poor children
whom waste their time
trying to find out
what everyone is saying.
Teach them young
that technology will fail you,
for all we have
and all that matters
is the time
on our
hands.

Addiction

It's a dirty word
because it assumes
you put yours above all else,
damn the consequences.
Sometimes there is no consequence.
When there is none,
you've found the one.

Poetry Pause

There will come a time
in your life when nothing else matters.
The make-up and
glitter lipstick is no longer a must.
You're educated now,
and your children have had, children.
Every plot is the same,
you're used to it by now.
Pause and write some poetry,
and don't be surprised at how talented you are.

So Still

Sometimes I am so still
I can sit with a squirrel
high in a tree.
So still, that the chickadee
contemplates friendship.
So still, that the mountain
of life is no longer on my shoulders.

I Killed The Fox

It was out of season
but I had this new gun, you see. It was him or me!
Men kill things they don't understand,
and when they see the dead for what it was,
they weep inside for what they've done.

Jim Harrison

I wish I could have met you and your eye.
Just so we could sit and talk about the Pope
or maybe have a shot of whiskey so
we could collaborate on a poem.
Both with Michigan roots,
and probably fed up with most humans,
we'd find comfort shooting a few rounds
and knocking back an expensive bottle of wine.
Thank you for all you've done for me,
despite our lack of introductions.

Anthony

Oh Anthony,
a smart college student
who found his sweetheart at a gas station.
She left him for a
homeless man
after bearing 3 children.
He's been hit by lightening
three times
and sleeps at his desk
waiting to die.

7's

Starting in your 7's
they start to become
catty.

When they do,
run off and find yourself
another.

Repeat this madness
in order to remain
happy.

Friends will come and go, keep the ones
that try as hard as you do.

How the World Works

To understand how the world works,
is to fall for the stories,
that the righteous have written.

It's no more glorious to become
a doctor of medicine
as it is to become a garbage man.

Understand that your journey in this life,
is how the world works.

Neil's Law

A young black man
who survived the riots
and walked through judgement
to rise to the very top
of an agency.
He is America.
He is hope.
He is my friend and I wish
this black man
could have been my father.
So pure in the heart,
and the parent of champions.
His lessons will be passed
on to my children and they will know,
to *own their space, and dress,*
for the position they want.

Comfort

Worried is the girl,
who checks her everything,
before anything.

Fear of judgement.

Fear of rumors.

Find your comfort zone, my sweet girl,
and thrive there -
where everything doesn't matter.

Experience

There should be a book written,
"If I knew then, what I know now."

No one would read it.

Warm Waves

The truth is revealed
by the sea,
when *she* wants to reveal it.

The ocean surely is a woman, you see,
so vast in her knowledge,
and easy to punish,
if you cross her.

Washing away your flesh
and exposing truth,
is what she'll do to you.

So be kind,
and take pictures of her
when she's beautiful.

But be patient when she's sad,
and wipe away her salt water,
when it runs down her cheek.

Missing

I constantly seem to be chasing you,
wondering where you are
in this irrational world we live in.

Dreaming one night of a thousand black post cards,
a seating chart for our travels.

All the spots are filled,
except for the one spot,
next to your name.

"GIVE ME THAT SEAT!", I beg the hostess.

She only nods, as I fall in slow motion,
desperately trying to hold on.

Talk

Doomed by the
shortening days
and lack of mojo,
my neck pulses in pain.

No falls
or accidental
mishaps
to blame.

One hemisphere
traded for another,
the mind hibernates in a dark dry place.

Very few methods
overcome these feelings
of despair.

Power down,
that which surrounds you,
and talk.

Fly, girl

Your spirit soars higher every day. So high, it's beyond the treetops where birds are curious and chirp encouragement to your every flip and flap. Here you will fit right in with our feathered friends. Only your species will judge you, and thankfully you are the endangered kind. Love yourself for the way you fly. Float away from others who spend their days nesting and cursing your adventures.

Television

If somehow you can avoid it,
please do. Live without television and you
can live with your own thoughts on social justice.
You'll be able to complete something in your lifetime
without it, and I can promise you, when you are ready for it, you'll
catch a re-run and thank me that you didn't see it the first time.
Instead, turn on a loop of opera, and don't mind that you can't
understand Italian.
Your creations will thrive, your art will peak, and your words will flow with love,
honesty, and passion that will only be yours – without influence from anyone or anything.

Halo

Your halo
stays with me,
many years later.

A perfect outline
on a soft feather pillow.

The dent from
your final sleep
still remains
as if you floated straight up
off the bed,
or perhaps disappeared
straight through the middle of it.

A sight no child should see
even if the child is now
a man.

Making mistakes
until the very end,
one last act
this child can't comprehend.

A Million Heartbeats

You're not alone,
you really aren't.

Just outside,
through the backdoor,
are a million heartbeats.

Go then, take a chair and sit in the woods.

Be as still as you can.
It will take hours for the woodsy
inhabitants to forget you're there.
A lifetime for them, I'm sure.

But be still dear, and you'll see.

Squirrels shake their fists at one another,
quarrel over food,
and fight over the best sticks for shelter
because almost all of them live alone.

The ugly female cardinals
fight each other on the ground
just below the pleasing eye
of the radiant red male.

As the sun sets a beautiful bushy red fox,
glides above the earth,
toward the farmers back yard.
Only the morning knows
if the rooster will crow.

Fold your chair now,
and know that you aren't alone.

Build your home,
even if you're alone.

Let the pretty boys
fight over you.

Save others from wrong,
and best of all,
live for you.

Prison Frames

Look at these poor souls
peering out of tiny
prison frames
of about 3 by 3.

The foreground full of masks and filters,
to boost approvals
and gather applause
the stats climb higher and higher.

Meanwhile,
the reality of the background
brings you to your knees.

Leave approvals
for the weak
and go
South.

Live like a wild one,
stay out of store front windows.

Grudges

I've held his hand for so many years,
keeping him out of traffic and
saving him from choking hazards, that finally,
I have become the choking hazard.

Let go of the grip and the grudges,
and let the vines sprawl to new lands.
After all, he is your wonder boy.

To your advice, Uncle, I thank you not once, not twice, but thrice.

Kind

To be kind to others,
is not to brag about,
or shout it from the pixelated mountains.
That's not pure, that's showboating!

Grab that check and pay it forward,
or feed a lost pigeon,
but don't break your arm patting yourself on the back.

Kindness knows no congratulatory ceremony
for all to admire. It's a karma point, to be tallied at
the end of your journey, no matter what you believe in.

Lost at Sea

Your boat is too big
for this harbor now,
no matter what
the land lubbers tell you
about her seaworthiness.

Push off from those old
weathered docks
that keep knocking you around
and ruining your hull,
trying to sink your mighty ship.

Paddle like hell!

Find your isle,
your buried treasure,
life's moral compass.

Know too, that we have
tried the voyage you're afraid to take,
and we have sunk many times before.

Chase the sunsets,
avoid the peg legs,
and keep rebuilding your ship until,
it floats.

Highschool Kids

Technology keeps us in high school
well into our 40's and beyond.

The same sweet people are there
and so are the idiots.

Unlike high school, you can expel
those who attend and create a perfect
bully-free zone.

Discover

Numb to the routine,
you'll forget most of your days,
unless you align yourself
with something so great and powerful
that every day seems like a re-birth
of curiosity and self-adventure.
The minute you care more about money
than you do about discovering you,
it's too late.

Logging Notes

The forest floor was too dark
to take a shot, and it felt much too early for this.
Grey on top of black on top of blurred vision,
reveals nothing to me at this moment.
But here's a second light,
a second chance at vision in these busy woods.
Straining to keep them wide,
I see limited movement of life,
in and out of heavenly beams of light.
Not far, just over there,
I see a family of ten pile out of a hallow log.
Slow moving and stumbling over one another
they prepare for their work-night.
None of them seem to mind that
no one has moved out of the house yet.

Powerful Pictures

These pictures are so suggestive
that all you need to do to remind someone,
to influence them,
or to tell them you love them
is to slide a lovely picture under the door.
The medium means nothing,
but the sentiment will last forever.

New Clothes

The hardest thing you'll ever do
is to clean out your closet and give away
those things you no longer need.

Good bye, things that make you feel fat
or too skinny.

Adios judgmental jeans and
jealous worn out belts keeping you
from being free and happy.

Pitch those,
that make you feel anything less than lovely.

Sunday's

Held close to his nose,
this old man carefully sorts his cards,
like they're the secret
to everlasting life.
Peering over his Kings and Queens
with sweat streaming down his face from his jet black greaser hair,
he rolls his tongue around his cigarette
and grips it with half a smirk.
The smell of an alcoholic – chemical pesticide and deodorant, skunked
beer, and Old Spice.
How did Dad stand this guy,
with his cotton white tank top
and Buddy Holly safety glasses?
Who plays cards outside in July anyway?
Why are we even here?
There aren't any kids to play with.
I don't have any toys here.
Isn't it Sunday? Shouldn't I be going home soon?
I'm so thirsty, all they have is water.
Nothing is on TV.
"Go play!", they tell me.
This is how it feels
for a child,
when you put yourself
before your children.
Live for them,
you made me.

1984

Pillow fights
and camping nights,
kick the can
and flashlight tag,
BB guns
and broken windows,
fist fights
and heroes,
sports stars
and candy bars,
Boston Coolers
and bike rides,
rock throwing
and girl watching,
musical stereo
and moon walks,
revenge of the nerds
and boob shots,
boys of summer
and sand lots,
my life wouldn't be the same
without these games.

Spidermom

These wolf spiders are relentless,
carrying a thousand children
on their backs until they're strong enough
to walk on their own 8 feet.

Robert

Robert was a bald
and monotone man
who raved about elections every four years
and was passionate about
reviewing films and sleeping at his desk
in the middle of the day.
He talked about his family
and his grown-up girls every day.
Once, he took a nap at his desk,
and never woke up.

Airmail

"I love you", on both wings of this paper airplane. So carefully, did I fold its structure. This flight was the biggest of my life. Out through a cracked window, the airplane flew across town, catching the Niagara airstream and landing at the feet of a child. I bet it's still flying somewhere in Canada.

Outer Crabs

Cranking the handle on
the spinning animations
I see the crab nip my foot and draw blood.
I enjoy the rush of living in that moment,
and help him back to sea.
Showing off my bloody stump,
proud of the way I have dealt with this
foe, I wonder if anyone cares?
Probably not, because who cares about this tiny crab
and my tiny scratch?
But forgiving what comes natural to this beast
is rewarding in some way.
If all natures enemies were
as innocent as this one,
we'd never have scars.

Made in the USA
Middletown, DE
26 October 2017